The ABC's of Happiness

NOT FOR CHILDREN

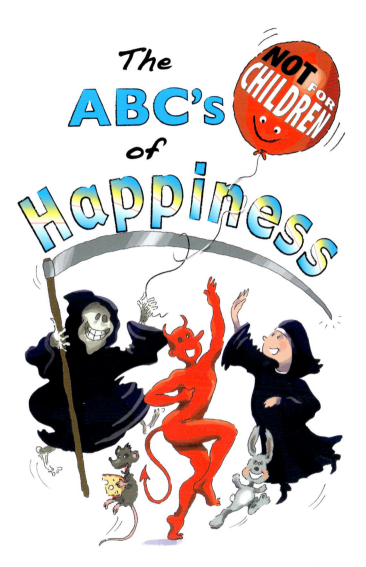

Mark Yablonovich *and* **Juliet Kaska**
illustrated by **Scot Ritchie**

WEST
VILLAGE
PRESS

To our parents

Introduction

Welcome to the lessons you never got in kindergarten. Here's your adult version of the ABC's along with some tips:

Action: This book was created for busy people. The exercises will take you 10 minutes a day and make a real difference in your life.

Backlash: When you start to change, your mind rebels. Relax, allow whatever feelings arise, bitch to your shrink and self-medicate with chocolate.

Community: Sure, you know working out and eating beans is a good idea but real change happens when you internalize lessons at a deeper level. We created the online meditations so the ABC's can sink into a place beyond your rational mind. You can find the meditations for each lesson at www.abcgiftbook.com.

Now jump in and have fun!

A is for Acceptance

Anne accepts a slower pace...

...Abe cannot accept his place

"I want out."

Stretch Your Mind

As human beings, we're constantly resisting the present moment and grasping for the next one. How do we move from resistance to acceptance? The key is to simply notice and allow "negative" states such as anger, sadness and resistance itself. This isn't condoning or being passive – it's creating space for real change in your life.

Move Your Pen

On the lines below, list some things about yourself you don't accept. Look at each one and say "I now choose to accept this." It's just an exercise – have fun with it.

Change Your Life

Meditation is the most powerful path to acceptance because it trains your mind to be in the present moment without trying to change it. Now stop and breathe. Notice what emotions arise and just let them be. *Online Meditation: Practice Acceptance.*

Notes

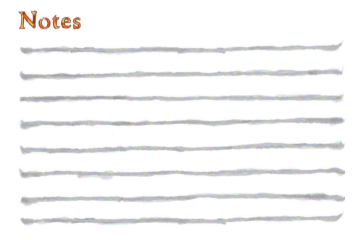

Inhale. Exhale. Repeat.

B is for Balance

Barb finds balance her own way...

"TGIF!"

...Bill can balance work and play

"Oooo, oooo, oooo, can I do this one, Dad?"

Stretch Your Mind

While riding your bicycle, taking a walk, playing with your dog, you may experience a sudden sense of balance. Your thoughts flow. Your mood lifts. You feel at home in the moment. You can experience more such moments by creating a balanced schedule.

Move Your Pen

Jot down the main areas of your life, such as work, family, sex, chocolate. What percentage of your time do you give to each? What's out of balance?

Change Your Life

Schedule a regular activity that gives you a sense of balance. Your mind might rebel here: "I have no time! You want me to quit my job? Neglect my kids? Watch less TV?*#!" Simply notice and allow that voice. Treat it like a member of your cabinet, not the President.

Online Meditation: Find Balance.

Notes

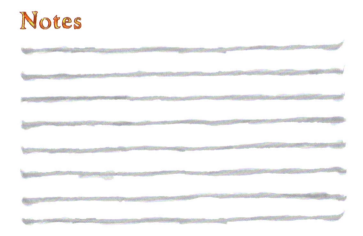

No bonus points for suffering.

 is for Creativity

Claire likes creating trouble...

"There once was a boy from Ur-Anus."

...Cal likes creating double

"He's impossible to work for. I hear there are two great openings you-know-where."

Stretch Your Mind

A sudden burst of creativity can take our breath away. We're creating something from nothing, bringing words, images, whole worlds into existence. Creativity seems to float up from a part of us we don't fully know. It's an act of will and an act of surrender. And then it's gone. Now stop and be still, noticing that space from which creativity arises.

Move Your Pen

List some things you want to create: A business plan. A love poem. A life that inspires you. Choose one and go for it.

Change Your Life

Combine focus and surrender to unleash creativity: write about an area you want creative solutions in and then switch to a rhythmic activity such as dancing and meditation. See what arises. *Online Meditation: Rejoice in Creativity.*

Notes

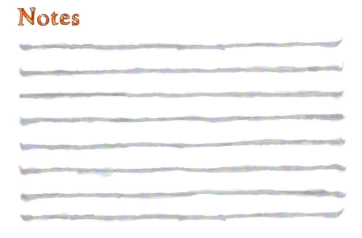

Create some new action scenes for
this movie called your life.

D is for Daring

Dasher's daring on the clock...

"WAY too much eggnog."

...Darren's daring with his flock

"You never want to experiment anymore."

Stretch Your Mind

The self-help gurus tell us to always take chances, be vulnerable, live on the edge. This inspires some people but just traumatizes others. Ignore the gurus and strike your own balance between comfort and growth. When you are present and centered, the appropriate level of daring will naturally present itself.

Move Your Pen

List some things you might do with your life if you dared to fail. Know that Abe Lincoln lost more elections than he won and that Babe Ruth was the "Home-Run King" *and* the "Strike-Out King."

Change Your Life

Do one thing outside your comfort zone. Bonus points for striking out or losing an election. *Online Meditation: Unleash Daring.*

Notes

Take baby steps or high dive. Just get in the water.

E is for Empathy

Emma's empathy has peaked...

"Now, now, I'm sure nothing you did is all that bad, dear."

...Edwin's empathy grows weak

"All they ever do is complain and ask for stuff."

Stretch Your Mind

A cute puppy or a national tragedy may open our hearts but, for the most part, we go through life shielded and armored. It's natural selection — we're rigged for fight or flight. Knowing your defenses will be there when you need them (and when you don't), you can begin to practice being open and empathetic.

Move Your Pen

List three people you dislike and your reasons. Now step inside their world — as you imagine it — and experience what life might be like for them.

Change Your Life

Next time you interact with someone difficult, sense what might lie behind their defenses. You don't need to say anything. Just be open and observe. And if you still find them to be a pain in the gluteus maximus (ass), that's fine too – see A is for Acceptance. *Online Meditation: Feel Empathy.*

Notes

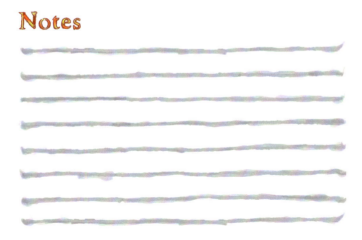

We all struggle and resist. We all suffer.

F is for **F**riendship

Friends help friends in times of need...

...Friends don't care about your breed

Stretch Your Mind

How's your friendship with the person you're with 24/7? Can you tell yourself anything? Do you enjoy spending quiet time with yourself? Do you appreciate your little quirks? Unless you're four (in which case put this book down right now!) you won't create a deep friendship with yourself overnight. So what's the first step going to be?

Move Your Pen

Recall times you experienced friendship and write down what it meant to you.

Change Your Life

Connect with an old friend. And, connect with you.
Online Meditation: Enjoy Friendship.

Notes

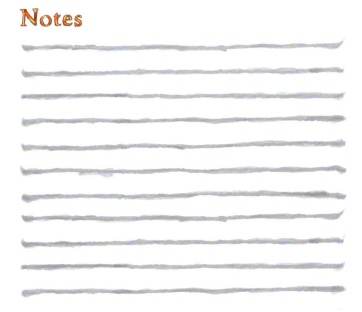

Friends let friends just be.

 G is for Gratitude

Gene's grateful for his paddle...

...Gwen's grateful in the Saddle

Stretch Your Mind

There are moments we feel spontaneously grateful. For the most part, though, gratitude is a state we cultivate. You may already be grateful for the pleasant things in life: "Thank you for my friends and family and for this morning's quadruple orgasm." How about the unpleasant stuff? "Thanks for deadlines and broccoli and annoying people." Gratitude is a choice and eventually a habit.

Move Your Pen

List some things you're grateful for and some you wish were different. For a moment, experience being grateful for everything on both your lists.

Change Your Life

In your own way, show someone you're grateful they're in your life. *Online Meditation: Express Gratitude.*

Notes

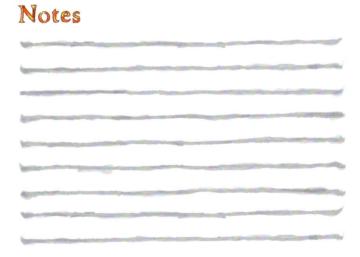

What would your life be like if
you saw *all* of it as a gift?

H is for Humility

Hanna's not a humble quail...

"Bitch had it coming."

...Harold's humble when he fails

"Perhaps we should've given sanctions
a little more time to work."

Stretch Your Mind

When we consider the vastness of the universe, aren't we like ants? Yet we live as if the thoughts in our head are the almighty. Pretty arrogant ants, no? Humility begins with waking up from the delusion that because you believe something it must be true.

Move Your Pen

List a few times in the past you were a bonehead.

Change Your Life

Say "Oops. I was dead wrong" three times today. For bonus points and a great life, say it three times every day.
Online Meditation: Embrace Humility.

Notes

Consider that you have **way** too many opinions.

I is for Inspiration

Inge's inspired by her job choice...

"Well, I have a real passion for working with people."

...Irv's inspired by his own voice

"Which brings me to my next point . . ."

Stretch Your Mind

When was the last time you felt inspired, exhilarated, giddy? How much of your day goes to things that make you feel alive? A little? A lot? None? When is that going to change?

Move Your Pen

List the things you'd be inspired to do if you had no constraints. Nothing is too big or too small. Sitting outside and "just" breathing counts. So does saving the world.

Change Your Life

Come on, try something new! Get a pet. Meditate. Join a band. Create some inspiration while you're still here. *Online Meditation: Live Inspiration.*

Notes

Check your pulse.

J is for Journey

Janice journeys to new plates...

...Jergen journeys to new states

"Just act normal, dear."

Stretch Your Mind

Every moment is a journey that we rarely notice. We live like there's someplace to get to but the joke's on us -- we're already there. Stop and breathe. Experience being inspired by your dreams and fully present for the journey.

Move Your Pen

Grab some colored pencils and draw your journey. The faraway palace. The winding road. Your allies and enemies. Pretend your life is a magical adventure.

Change Your Life

Plan a trip across town and on that trip journey inward. *Online Meditation: Take a Journey.*

Notes

Go on a long walk—coming back is optional.

K is for **K**indness

Kenny's kind to lost strangers...

"You're lucky I'm on that all-carb diet this week!"

...Kim's kindness is in danger

"Wanna catch the end of my ex-husband's funeral?"

Stretch Your Mind

Kindness is a way of looking at the world. You can be kind to yourself, to another, to a piece of wood. Kindness is hard to force when you're rushed and stressed out. When you slow down, kindness has space to naturally arise.

Move Your Pen

List some ways you can be kind to yourself and others.

Change Your Life

Close your eyes, allow a gentle half-smile to form on your face and say "may I be filled with kindness." Now send this wish to someone you care about and then to someone you have difficulty with. *Online Meditation: Be Kind.*

Notes

Kindness feels good.

L is for Laughter

Larry laughs so hard it hurts...

"And then he says to his friend, 'I don't need to outrun the bear, I just need to outrun you.'"

...Lois laughs until it squirts

"Stop! You're killing me."

Stretch Your Mind

Do you ever play like a three year old? Or do you walk around with that "I'm a grownup" frown stapled to your face? Laughter is healing. The great teacher Alan Watts once said the survival of the human race depends on our ability to have fun. Ponder that one.

Move Your Pen

List some things that bring out the kid in you: your friend Betty, her dog, a movie that made you laugh. Not smile ironically. Laugh.

Change Your Life

Design a few ways to have a good laugh once a day.
Online Meditation: Awaken Laughter.

Notes

Let yourself have some fun. We already know how this all ends.

 is for Mind

Mindy's mind won't be controlled...

"When are you gonna leave the farmer, baby?"

...Morton's mind can quickly fold

"I guess if all your friends are doing it."

Stretch Your Mind

Do you want to experience more joy? Greater effectiveness? Better sex? Chances are, you keep trying to change your external circumstances. What if you focused instead on your inner programming?

Move Your Pen

Describe the sort of mind that would allow you to create the life you want. A mind that's calm, creative, kind?

Change Your Life

On the site, we list powerful resources to help you gently and gradually rewire your mind. Choose one.
Online Meditation: Master Mind.

Notes

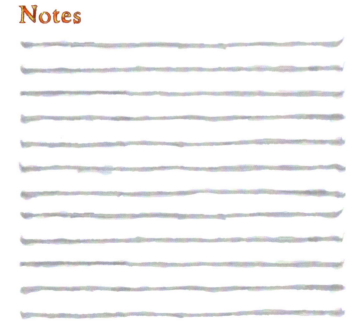

Observe your mind at work. Pretty scary, huh?

 is for Noticing

Nell now notices the score...

"You'll hop into bed with any floozy."

...Ned just noticed a new sore

"That's weird — Nancy has one of these too."

Stretch Your Mind

Human beings live on auto-pilot most of the time. How much of your life do you notice? Not analyze and dissect – notice. Real noticing is being present in the moment. You feel the sadness. You see the grasshopper. You taste the strawberry.

Move Your Pen

Jot down your current emotions. Now stop and simply be with them. Notice how the experience of life is constantly changing, infinitely vast, incapable of being captured with words.

Change Your Life

Pick up a guided meditation CD and register for a half-day retreat. *Online Meditation: Value Noticing.*

Notes

Notice something. Keep noticing even
as thoughts try to pull you away.

 **is for O**penness

Oscar's open to good news...

"Congratulations, human. You have been selected to come with us to a much better place."

...Olga's open to all views

"Oh dear, what would Satan do?"

Stretch Your Mind

Life is throbbing, flowing, exploding all around us. We filter most of it out. This constant pushing away is draining. Just on the other side of our resistance lies a universe of freedom, joy and possibility.

Move Your Pen

List things, people and beliefs you're closed off to, even a little. Now look at your list and, for a moment, let your tension and resistance melt.

Change Your Life

Explore something that might expand the way you look at the world. A murder mystery? Tribal dance? Shamanic journeying? Go way beyond your comfort zone.
Online Meditation: Risk Openness.

Notes

Just a crazy idea: try something new.

P is for Practice

Preus practices his pitch...

"'You look tasty, human.' No, no, that won't work.
How about 'Congratulations, human. You have been
selected to come with us to a much better place.'"

...Peggy practices her stitch

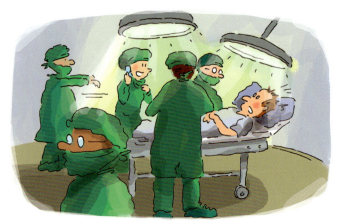

"This is the coolest internship ever! We're gonna
do a vasectomy today."

Stretch Your Mind

Do you think you'd have a healthy mouth if you brushed your teeth once a year? As a culture, we look for the quick fix instead of regular practices that cause real change. We all have automatic practices: breathing, complaining, drinking nineteen sodas a day. These practices give us a certain life. You can create a new life by choosing new practices.

Move Your Pen

List some things in your life you'd like to improve this year. They can be skills like dancing the polka or personality traits such as acceptance, wisdom and humor.

Change Your Life

Now choose two things from your list and create a regular practice for each, such as breathing into your emotions once an hour and playing your guitar every Friday night. *Online Meditation: Go Practice.*

Notes

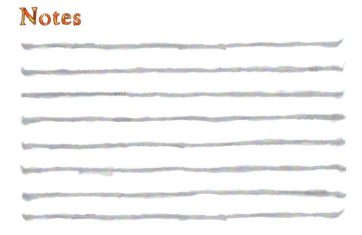

Give yourself permission to
make mistakes. Big ones.

 **is for Questions**

Quentin's questions aren't so great...

"Did I die and go to heaven?"

...Quila more than questions fate

"Just open the gates, darling, and nobody gets hurt."

Stretch Your Mind

We're asking questions all the time: "What will they think?" "Will this hurt?" "Why me?" Questions focus our attention and our actions. If you want to create new results, start asking new questions.

Move Your Pen

Write down three questions that can improve your life. For example: "What are five ways to solve this problem?" "What's the best use of my time today?" "How do I get my hands on that piece of cake?" Now brainstorm possible answers to one of your questions.

Change Your Life

Set aside five minutes a day and make this exercise part of your life. *Online Meditation: Love Questions.*

Notes

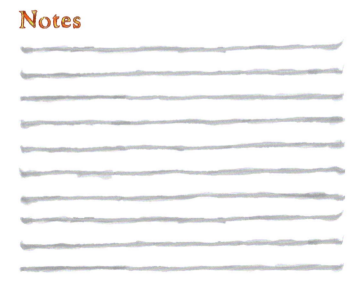

Question your most basic assumption:
who you think you are.

R is for Release

Roz releases many squeals...

"Someone call the health department!"

...Ron releases how he feels

"If I read ONE MORE thing about omega 3 being good for you . . . just let it go Ron, let it go."

Stretch Your Mind

You've experienced them before: moments of letting go. They come with a feeling of freedom and joy. When you release the need to control your life, strange and wonderful things arise. Like peace, creativity and love.

Move Your Pen

List some habits, beliefs and relationships you may be ready to release.

Change Your Life

Give away old clothes you'll never wear. Throw away the moldy cheese. Gently surrender your old and moldy thoughts. *Online Meditation: Allow Release.*

Notes

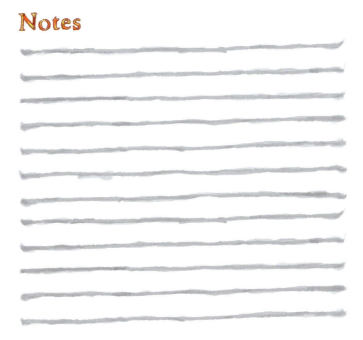

Pretend you have amnesia.

S is for Stillness

Samuel's still before his lunch...

"Thank you, Lord, for this meal we are about to receive."

...Sarah's stillness sparks a hunch

"I don't think he's really looking for work."

Stretch Your Mind

Stop and listen. Sense the stillness just below the surface. Our problems disappear when we're still. What percent of your day is spent in such a state? 20%? 10%? 1%? Be still and let that number sink in.

Move Your Pen

Take two minutes to just be. Nothing to do. Just relax and breathe. Allow whatever arises. Now see what words, shapes or images appear on the lines below.

Change Your Life

Make stillness part of your life.
Online Meditation: Welcome Stillness.

Notes

Stop.

T is for Trust

Thomas trusts they'll see the light...

"Mr. Smith, do you think you're the only lawyer in town interested in selling his soul?"

...Thea trusts the future's bright

"Global cooling, global schmooling.
Feels plenty warm to me."

Stretch Your Mind

Pretend you're a character in a movie and simply take the next step in the story. Does all that mental chatter really help you? What if you trusted life, not because there are guarantees everything will be okay, but because constant struggle sucks and gets you nowhere.

Move Your Pen

List things that worry you. Look at each one and say "I trust this will work out perfectly – no matter how it works out."

Change Your Life

Remind yourself daily to look at your life as a movie. Can you stop talking and enjoy the show for a while?
Online Meditation: Expand Trust.

Notes

Imagine your worst-case scenario.
Now imagine fully allowing it.

U is for Unity

Uma unites with what's green...

"Somebody get this #!@*&^$ woman off me!"

...Uri unites with his machine

"We should do date night more often, honey."

Stretch Your Mind

We go through life feeling separate. The sages say this is a terrible illusion and we're all one. That's a valuable perspective. At some level, though, we are separate and that too can be wonderful. How can you savor an apple pie or a walk on the beach or falling in love if you stop being a separate entity? You enjoy these things because of the mix of separation and unity. Be grateful for both.

Move Your Pen

Draw two circles and a triangle. Simply look at them for a while. See what thoughts about unity and separation arise.

Change Your Life

Be part of something larger than yourself. Nature? Church choir? Nudist camp? Follow your passion.

Online Meditation: Experience Unity.

Notes

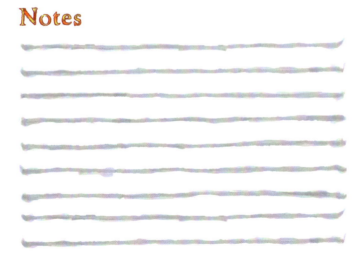

All is one. And many.

V is for Values

Vickie values family meals...

"Compliment mom on the stew, babe. It's an emotional roller coaster slow-cooking your fourth husband."

...Vincent values being real

"What the #!*% are you looking at? I've got 17 mouths to feed plus alimony!"

Stretch Your Mind

If a friendly visitor from Uranus looked at your day-to-day life, what would they think you valued? Does your life reflect your deepest values or your fears, habits and compulsions?

Move Your Pen

Revisit the chapter on Inspiration. What values can you extract from the things that inspire you? Going to Paris and skydiving might both suggest you value adventure. Notice if you're leaving out values you "shouldn't" have, such as sensuality or recognition or power.

Change Your Life

Every week, take one of your values and choose a new way to express it. *Online Meditation: Uncover Values.*

Notes

How will you use your remaining time here?

W is for **W**ords

Wanda's words change others' lives...

"Have you considered creating an inauthentic
self so people will like you more?"

...William's words can cut like knives

"I'm sorry, I just don't think we're on the
same wavelength anymore."

Stretch Your Mind

Notice the difference between saying over and over "I can do what I set my mind to" versus "I'm not doing well." Now notice the difference between both of these and silence.

Move Your Pen

Observe your internal dialogue and jot down some things you say to yourself. Pick one conversation and let it go. If it comes back, don't fight it or try to displace it with positive thinking. Just notice it and smile.

Change Your Life

Practice deep silence. You'll feel centered. Others will be drawn to you. *Online Meditation: Forget Words.*

Notes

Who told you to listen to the voices in your head?

X is for Xanadu

Dreams of Xanadu fill Xun...

...Xena's Xanadu's more fun

Stretch Your Mind

Kubla Khan

by Samuel Taylor Coleridge

In Xanadu did Kubla Khan
A stately pleasure-dome decree:
Where Alph, the sacred river, ran
Through caverns measureless to man
Down to a sunless sea.
So twice five miles of fertile ground
With walls and towers were girdled round:
And there were gardens bright with sinuous rills,
Where blossomed many an incense-bearing tree;
And here were forests ancient as the hills,
Enfolding sunny spots of greenery.

Move Your Pen

On the lines below, create your own magical place.

Change Your Life

Read aloud and with passion the poem excerpted above.
Online Meditation: Discover Xanadu.

Notes

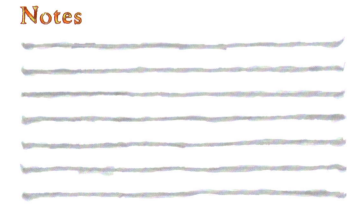

Take a day off from your everyday life.

Y is for Yes

Yale says yes to mental health...

...Yvonne says yes to greater wealth

"If it dips below 17, definitely buy."

Stretch Your Mind

Yes is not an intellectual judgment about your life circumstances. It's surrendering to the perfection of this moment. Suffering exists in the realm of thinking and resistance. There may be pain in this moment but no suffering. Be with your breath fully for a few moments and see for yourself. Your inhale is perfect just as it is. So is your exhale.

Move Your Pen

List the things you say yes to. Want to change anything on your list?

Change Your Life

For one minute, celebrate all of life – the traffic jam, the little pain that's been bothering you, the crazy thoughts in your head. *Online Meditation: Say Yes.*

Notes

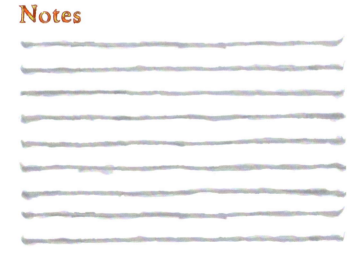

Say yes to what? How about everything?

 **is for Zest**

Zander's zest for life is gone...

"I always thought this would make me happy."

...Zelda's zest is far from done

Stretch Your Mind

There's a powerful aliveness inside you. It may need to be excavated -- with a shovel or maybe an oil rig. The lessons in this book are your tools. Use them.

Move Your Pen

What are you passionate about? Writing a book, moving to Manhattan, breeding otters? Be honest with yourself.

Change Your Life

Choose to live a life full of zest. No positive thinking here. Sadness and anger are fine. So are naps. But you know what we mean. Choose a life of zest. *Online Meditation: Renew Zest.*

Notes

Relax. You don't need to work
it all out in this lifetime.

Sharing the ABC's

Acknowledge: We'd love your praise! Please write a review online.

Buy: Hanukkah. Christmas. Full moon. It's perfect for any occasion.

Commit: Let this book transform your life – that's the best way to share it with others. Redo the exercises. Form a book group. Subscribe to the ABC's of Happiness newsletter. And, crazy as it sounds, let it be fun.

www.abcgiftbook.com

Your Daily ABC's

The practices below will help you through some tough moments and, over time, change your life.

You can cut this page out or print it at www.abcgiftbook.com.

Allow: Close your eyes and simply notice the emotions and sensations in your body. Welcome them. Anger, fear, resistance, excitement – allow yourself just 10 seconds every hour to fully experience your life without trying to control it.

Breathe: Follow the rise and fall of your breath, letting it take you deeper and deeper into the perfection of the present moment.

Create: On your next breath, allow your current emotions as you inhale and create a new experience as you exhale. Play with different possibilities: joy, surrender, love.

Let these exercises be part of your daily life and notice the gentle and profound transformation in yourself over time.

Acknowledgments

You wouldn't be very happy right now if you had read the first draft of this book. So here's to all the people who contributed to The ABC's: Our editor, Gali Kronenberg; our cover designer, Joyce Turley; our typesetter, Sue Balcer; Sam Pigott, who guided this project from beginning to end.

The following people gave us great feedback at various stages: Kate Anderson, Paulina Anne, Trudi Aviles, Monica Balderrama, Simone Bricci, Jennifer Brockett, Sean Cartwright, Deanna Danski, Isadora Delgado, Michelle DeRouen, David Dubin, Kirstin Durran, Matt Dundon, Evette Giddens, Kenny Golding, Constance Goodwin, Tonya Greer, Jason Hendler, Linda Johnston, Pauletta Kaufman, Ben Keepers, Paul Locker, Tanya Lugo, Anna Lyndon, Jon Lynn, Josh Lynn, Robert Martin, Lara McGlashan, Alida Meksavanh, Mindy Myers, Lucretia Patterson, Camille Pincham-Jones, Marc Primo, Sarah Rocha, Amy Rubin, Ashley Shearrion, Christine Slapik, Eric Stahl, Noah Stein, Susan Strong, Katherine Tighe, Sarah Vesecky, Alexis Van Pelt, Barbara Way, Lidia Yablonovich, Yakov Yablonovich.

Juliet would like to thank her friends and the team at Emerson Hall Fitness who contributed to this book and to her life and special thanks to her parents, Barbara Perreault, Charles Kaska + Stepmom Patricia Gambino, grandmother Flornece Powers Kaska and angel Grandma "blondie." And most of all to the one being who is her happiness and joy in every moment of life, Cali The Rat.

Juliet Kaska Juliet Kaska is one of the nation's premiere fitness experts. In 2008, she became the fitness expert on NBC's "Extra." Juliet has been featured in or contributed to The Dr. Phil Show, Good Morning America, E! News, Access Hollywood, Good Day LA, Vogue, W magazine, SELF, Shape, Seventeen, Fitness RX, People, Oxygen, US Weekly and more. Juliet is the owner of Emerson Hall Fitness, a boutique fitness studio in West Hollywood, CA. Her series of mini- "Red Carpet Ready" videos are available at www.exercisetv.tv. www.julietkaska.com

Scot Ritchie is an award–winning illustrator who has been drawing and writing for over 20 years. He has worked with everybody from The Wall St. Journal to the National Film Board of Canada. He has illustrated 40 books, 7 of which he also wrote. Scot's books have been translated into Korean, Dutch, French and Polish. www.scotritchie.com

Mark Yablonovich graduated from Harvard Law School and built one of California's top employment class action law firms. He then pursued his passion for bringing meditation to the workplace and now leads meditation and stress reduction seminars for organizations across the United States. www.clearinsightgroup.com

The Serious Stuff

The ABC's of Happiness: Not for Children

By Juliet Kaska and Mark Yablonovich
Illustrations by Scot Ritchie

Visit our website: www.abcgiftbook.com

WEST VILLAGE PRESS

West Village Press, a division of Clear Insight Group, LLC
100 Wilshire Boulevard, Suite 950
Santa Monica, CA 90401

Yablonovich, Mark.

    The ABC's of happiness : (not for children) / Mark Yablonovich and Juliet Kaska ; illustrations by Scot Ritchie. -- Santa Monica, Calif. : West Village Press, c2008.

        p. ; cm.
        ISBN: 978-0-9816289-0-5

      1. Happiness--Popular works. 2. Happiness--Humor. 3. Attitude (Psychology)--Popular works. 4. Mental health--Popular works. I. Kaska, Juliet. II. Ritchie, Scot. III. Title.

BF575.H27 Y33 2008   2008924965
158.1--dc22   0804

Typesetting by JustYourType.biz
Cover design and layout by Joyce M. Turley, Dixon Cove Design

Printed and bound in Canada